PRESENTED TO:

my mom, Doris Hoyt
Love you!

You are a chosen people, a royal priesthood, a holy nation, a

people belonging to God, that you may declare the praises of

him who called you out of darkness into his wonderful light.

1 PETER 2:9

PRESENTED BY:

Diane Nash

DATE:

5/12/13

CHOSEN BY GOD

Harrison House
Tulsa, Oklahoma

You have been placed on this earth, at this particular time, for a very important reason. God has a purpose for your life—a very specific and significant calling for you to fulfill. And He longs to guide you along the best pathway for your journey.

Let the words of this book encourage you to draw near to Him. Ask Him to make clear His plans for you. Then ask Him for the strength and courage to fulfill that calling and hold firm in the belief that you have been *chosen by God.*

ot only has God chosen you to be His child, and adopted you into His wonderful family, He has made amazing promises to you in His Word, promises that He is committed to fulfilling in your life. And He has not only made these promises, but He stands *ready* to perform them, to make them come to pass in incredible, sometimes surprising, ways.

God, who cannot, and does not lie, has promised you that His goodness and mercy will follow you, His child, all the days of your life. All He asks is that you trust Him.

God has chosen to bless you—and if you're ready, He is too.

Then the Lord said to me, "You have seen well, for I am ready to perform My word."

JEREMIAH 1:12 NKJV

DECLARATION FOR YOUR LIFE

The Lord watches over His Word to see that it is performed in my life.

The Secret of Life

he famous English sculptor Henry Moore was asked a fascinating question by literary critic Donald Hall. "Now that you are eighty, you must know the secret of life. What is it?"

Henry Moore paused ever so slightly, with just enough time to smile before answering. "The secret of life," he mused, "is to have a task, something you do your entire life, something you bring everything to, every minute of the day for your whole life. And the most important thing is: It must be something you cannot possibly do."

God has a plan for your life, and He has chosen you for this very special task. The thing is, however, it will not be anything you can do on your own. As you rely on Him and His power working through you, you will accomplish more than you ever dreamed possible.

But the Lord said unto me, Say not, I am a child: for thou shalt go to all that I shall send thee, and whatsoever I command thee thou shalt speak. Be not afraid of their faces: for I am with thee to deliver thee, saith the Lord.

JEREMIAH 1:7–8 KJV

DECLARATION FOR YOUR LIFE

I will go everywhere the Lord sends me and do whatever He commands me to do. I do not allow fear to hinder me in my calling. I know full well that God's power is within me wherever I go and there is nothing that can overcome me.

he team captains are down to their last grudging choices: a slow kid for catcher and someone to stick out in right field where nobody hits the ball. They choose the last ones two at a time—"you and you"—because it makes no difference. And the remaining kids they deal for as handicaps: "If I take him, then you gotta take him," they say.

Did you ever think about the fact that you are so valuable to God that He "chose you early"—with enthusiasm? If God is for you, who could possibly be against you?

If ye were of the world, the world would love his own: but because ye are not of the world, but I have chosen you out of the world, therefore the world hateth you.

JOHN 15:19 KJV

DECLARATION FOR YOUR LIFE

I am not of this world. I have been chosen out of the world and am no longer subject to its ways of living and being. I have become one with Him in all things, and I follow Him with my whole heart.

s God's chosen son or daughter, you can come to the total assurance that God loves you, God knows where you are every second of every day, and God is bigger than any problem that life's circumstances can throw at you. You can have complete confidence that God is able to take care of any situation and provide an answer to any question or problem—He has all the resources of the universe to draw upon in helping you through any type of crisis, if you will trust in Him.

God delights in showing you again and again that He is the Source of your strength, your provision, your protection, and your ultimate success in life. You can have absolute assurance that God is in control of every second of your future—and He has a great future planned for you.

The Lord appeared from old to me [Israel],
saying, Yes, I have loved you with an
everlasting love; therefore with loving-
kindness have I drawn you and continued
My faithfulness to you.

JEREMIAH 31:3 AMP

DECLARATION FOR YOUR LIFE

*My heavenly Father loves me with an eternal devotion
and has drawn me to Himself with immeasurable
compassion. I have His word that He will mold me
and make me what He desires me to be. From here on
out, He will do nothing but encourage, strengthen, and
build me up. I can rest assured that He will never give
up on me. Therefore, I can now, at this present time,
take my place and dance with joy among the faithful.*

here were hundreds—maybe even thousands—of trained Israelite soldiers who were much more qualified to do battle with Goliath than David. But their response to Goliath's threats was paralyzing fear, stress, and frustration.

David, on the other hand, didn't seem to be upset at all. Why? Because it was God's battle, not his. Apart from the Lord, he knew he didn't stand a chance. But with the help of the Lord, he was confident that everything would turn out all right.

It's the same way in your life. Without God, you can do nothing; but with Him at your side, you are protected from the enemy's attack and empowered to be all that He has called you to be.

You hem me in—behind and before;
　　you have laid your hand upon me.

PSALM 139:5

DECLARATION FOR YOUR LIFE

The Spirit of my Father hems me in on all sides. His hand goes before me and guards my back as well. I live within His hedge of protection and the devil cannot get to me no matter how hard he tries.

GOD IS FAITHFUL

rchbishop of Calcutta Henry D'Sousza knows that at times in her life, Mother Teresa felt abandoned by God. He said that in one letter, she wrote that she had been walking the streets of Calcutta searching for a house where she could start her work. At the end of the day, she wrote in her diary, "I wandered the streets all day. My feet are aching, and I have not been able to find a home. And I also get the Tempter telling me, 'Leave all this, go back to the convent from which you came.'"

But God had not abandoned her. She found her home, and the rest is history. The Missionaries of Charity feeds 500,000 families a year in Calcutta alone, treats 90,000 leprosy patients annually, and educates 20,000 children every year.

What has God called you to do? As you follow Him, He will be faithful to fulfill His purpose in your life.

The Lord will perfect that which concerns
me; Your mercy and loving-kindness,
O Lord, endure forever—forsake not
the works of Your own hands.

PSALM 138:8 AMP

DECLARATION FOR YOUR LIFE

*No matter what has happened, the Lord will not
abandon me. He is faithful and will fulfill His purpose
for my life.*

here was once an old preacher who told some of his Sunday school boys the subject of his next Sunday's sermon. Wanting to trick him, the boys stole away with his Bible and glued some of the pages together. The next Sunday, the preacher stood to read his text. As he got to the bottom of the page he read, "When Noah was 120 years old he took unto himself a wife, who . . ." And turning the page he continued, ". . . was 140 cubits long, forty cubits wide, built of gopher wood, and covered with pitch inside and out."

The minister paused, a puzzled expression covering his face. He read it again, and then said, "My friends, this is the first time I have ever seen this in the Bible, but I take it as evidence of the assertion that we are fearfully and wonderfully made!"

You may not be made of gopher wood and covered with pitch, but God has created you as a very special and unique person! And He has a great destiny planned for your life.

I praise you because I am fearfully and
    wonderfully made;
  your works are wonderful,
  I know that full well.

PSALM 139:14

DECLARATION FOR YOUR LIFE

*I am fearfully and wonderfully made, and God is very
proud to call me His child. My thoughts of myself are
pure and positive. I know that I am a very special and
unique individual with a grand purpose and destiny
in this life.*

CALLED AND EQUIPPED

think for a moment about a carpenter who is getting ready to build a house. He has the blueprints in hand. He has acquired all of the materials necessary, including all of the lumber. Then he looks at his tools and says, "For this particular job, I need a hammer." And he pulls out a hammer and begins to use it.

In a similar fashion, God had a job in mind that needed to be done this year, in your particular area of the world, of the country, of your state, of your town. He created you to be His tool, His instrument, His vessel in getting that job done. From your birth, He has made you to be fully equipped, fashioned, and prepared for doing the job He had planned for you to do.

Being confident of this very thing, that He who has begun a good work in you will complete it until the day of Jesus Christ.

PHILIPPIANS 1:6 NKJV

DECLARATION FOR YOUR LIFE

I rest in full confidence that He who began this good work in me is well able to carry it on to completion until the day of Christ Jesus.

hrist in me is the ultimate proclamation of self-value! One of your purposes in this life is to demonstrate Christ, the hope of glory, who lives in you, to those you come in contact with.

The person who has a deep and abiding sense of self-worth can hear all kinds of criticism and cutting remarks from other people and let the negative comments just slide off him. He can go about his life's work with joy because he has an inner confidence that says, "So much for your opinion. I know *God* loves me, and His opinion of my value never diminishes, never changes, and is the only opinion that truly counts." Your critics, your detractors, and your enemies have no hold on you when you draw your identity, your help, and your sense of worth from God Himself.

Christ in you [is] the hope of glory.

COLOSSIANS 1:27

DECLARATION FOR YOUR LIFE

I proclaim the mystery that was hidden throughout the ages, but has now been made known to me. God has chosen me to make known the glorious riches of this mystery, which is Christ in me, the hope of glory.

od desires for us to become all that He has created us to be. He expects us to develop and then to use all of the talents, abilities, and gifts that He has placed within us. He intends for us to maximize our potential—to become the man or woman He created us to be.

God's plan is for us to accomplish all of the work that He sets before us. He does not call us to unfinished tasks or halfhearted ventures. When God places a challenge, opportunity, or goal in front of us, He expects us to pursue it with our whole heart, mind, and soul—to do so with strength and courage—and to experience His success in accomplishing what He has called us to do.

Be strong and of a good courage: for unto this people shalt thou divide for an inheritance the land, which I sware unto their fathers to give them. Only be thou strong and very courageous, that thou mayest observe to do according to all the law, which Moses my servant commanded thee: turn not from it to the right hand or to the left, that thou mayest prosper whithersoever thou goest.

JOSHUA 1:6–7 KJV

DECLARATION FOR YOUR LIFE

I will be strong and courageous. I have complete confidence in God's ability to give me the victory. I encounter danger and difficulties with firmness and without fear. I am bold, brave, and resolute. I fulfill my calling in a spirit of valor and determination that overcomes any obstacle that the enemy would put in my path.

few years ago, a family attended a Star Trek convention, marveling at all the fans dressed up as characters from the television series. One fan, who was costumed as a half-black-half-white alien, caught four-year-old Rebecca's eye. Thinking of her favorite children's chorus, "Jesus Loves the Little Children," she remarked, "Jesus thinks that one is precious." Then she added hopefully, "Do you think we'll see any red and yellows?"

No matter who you are or the color of your skin, God adores you and has chosen you as His child. Just as He created all the people of the world, He created you for a specific purpose, which He is committed to carrying out in your life!

Blessed are those you choose
    and bring near to live in your courts!
We are filled with the good things of
      your house,
    of your holy temple.
You answer us with awesome deeds
      of righteousness,
    O God our Savior,
the hope of all the ends of the earth
    and of the farthest seas.

PSALM 65:4–5

DECLARATION FOR YOUR LIFE

My Father has chosen me and adopted me as His own child. He has brought me near to Himself and has given me a place of honor in the courts of His palace. He fills me with all good things so that I am in need of nothing. All I have to do is ask and He freely gives me all that He has.

od never intended for His children to
live a life characterized by defeat. He
doesn't expect you to live in defeat in
your thought life, your emotions, your attitudes, your
self-control, or your faith. He paid much too high a
price to allow you into His family just to watch you
fail in your attempts to function as His family member.
He loves you too much to allow you to fail!

God's plan of salvation includes a provision to
help you accomplish all that He sets out for you to do.
And the key player in that part of His plan is the Holy
Spirit. The Holy Spirit is God's provision for righteous
living. He is the abiding presence of Christ's life within
you. That is why Paul could continue pressing on to
take hold of the prize—and why you can too!

Not that I have already obtained all this,
or have already been made perfect, but
I press on to take hold of that for which
Christ Jesus took hold of me.

PHILIPPIANS 3:12

DECLARATION FOR YOUR LIFE

*I never forget that I am saved from sin, not to sin. I do
not claim to be walking in the completeness of my
perfection in my present human condition, but I press
on to take hold of it, for this is the reason for which
Christ Jesus took hold of me.*

Pressing On

t the time you accepted Jesus Christ as your Savior, God gave you certain spiritual gifts to use in ministry to others. The way in which you express those gifts is uniquely linked to the talents He has given you and the skills He wants to help you develop. Paul told Timothy: "Do not neglect the gift which is in you" (1 Timothy 4:14 AMP). He also told the Philippians to press on toward the goal, the prize to which God had called them. (Philippians 3:14.)

Nobody who has lived before you has been exactly like you. No one alive on the earth today is exactly like you, not even a sibling who is your twin. Nobody who will ever live will be exactly like you, including your children. You are a unique and very special creation of God, designed for a particular purpose on this earth that God had in mind from eternity past. Accept who God made you to be and press on toward the prize!

Brothers, I do not consider myself yet to have taken hold of it [my purpose]. But one thing I do: Forgetting what is behind and straining toward what is ahead, I press on toward the goal to win the prize for which God has called me heavenward in Christ Jesus.

PHILIPPIANS 3:13–14

DECLARATION FOR YOUR LIFE

I forget what is behind me and press forward with my eyes on the prize of my high calling in Christ Jesus. I never let my past, whether five years ago or five minutes ago, hinder me in my walk with God. I am always moving forward, getting better with every step and staying in fellowship with my heavenly Father.

o you believe that God is surprised by any need that you experience? Do you believe that there is anything that His strength cannot enable you to handle? Do you believe that your sudden lack in a certain area of your life is either a mystery or a surprise to God? To the contrary— God knows you far better than you will ever know yourself. He knew about every need in your life long before you were ever conceived in your mother's womb. Not only did God know about that need, but He knew what His provision would be to meet that need.

Just as your need is no surprise and no mystery to Him, neither is the provision for solving your problem or meeting your need hidden from His understanding or ability. You have strength for all things in Christ—who empowers you.

I have strength for all things in Christ
Who empowers me [I am ready for
anything and equal to anything through
Him Who infuses inner strength into me;
I am self-sufficient in Christ's sufficiency].

PHILIPPIANS 4:13 AMP

DECLARATION FOR YOUR LIFE

The secret is this: I can do all things through the power of Christ that is in me. With His anointing, there isn't a single circumstance that can hold me down! I am self-sufficient in His sufficiency.

ong before you were ever conceived in your mother's womb, long before you took your first breath, spoke your first word, took your first step, God knew you and loved you so much that He set in motion a plan that would allow you to be with Him forever.

Long before you ever sinned, God set the rescue plan in motion—Jesus came to this earth and died so that you could live with God forever. You are cherished, deeply loved by the Creator of the universe, and He wants you to spend all of eternity with Him. All He asks is that you believe in Him and entrust the reins of your heart and life into His loving hands. Now, that's good news!

Behold what manner of love the Father
has bestowed on us, that we should
be called children of God!

1 JOHN 3:1 NKJV

DECLARATION FOR YOUR LIFE

*How great is the Father's love for me that I should
be called the son/daughter of God! And that is what
I am!*

THE MOST VALUABLE DISCOVERY

n 1847 Sir James Simpson was a doctor in Edinburgh, Scotland, when he discovered chloroform, one of the most significant discoveries in modern medicine.

Some years later after a lecture, a student asked him, "What do you consider to be the most valuable discovery of your lifetime?"

He answered, "My most valuable discovery was when I discovered myself a sinner and that Jesus Christ was my Savior."

The most valuable decision you will ever make is to accept Jesus as the Lord and Savior of your life. He has chosen you—won't you choose Him in return?

What things were gain to me,
those I counted loss for Christ.

PHILIPPIANS 3:7 KJV

DECLARATION FOR YOUR LIFE

*Any good that I find within me that comes from my
own power is worthless to me. I have set it all aside,
putting absolutely no trust in it, so that I can have the
overwhelming blessing of knowing my Lord Jesus.*

CHOSEN TO SHARE JESUS

n Algeria, a female Christian worker, who spoke Arabic well, would often engage a certain man in conversation about the divinity of Jesus, His mission to save us, and our need to submit to Him.

One particular day, after a lively dialogue, the woman was unable to respond further to his arguments. Smiling, he seemed pleased to think that no one could persuade him to accept Christ. Then, quietly, the woman began to cry.

Concerned, he asked, "Aren't you well? What is the matter?"

"Nothing," she replied. "It's because of your reluctance to recognize God's love for you."

He was deeply moved by her reaction. After a moment of silence he said, "A religion which moves someone to tears over someone else's spiritual welfare must be authentic." He then chose to accept Jesus as Savior.

Just as this woman did, you have been chosen to share God's love with the people He has placed in your life.

Go ye therefore, and teach all nations,
baptizing them in the name of the Father, and
of the Son, and of the Holy Ghost: Teaching
them to observe all things whatsoever I have
commanded you: and, lo, I am with you
alway, even unto the end of the world.

MATTHEW 28:19–20 KJV

DECLARATION FOR YOUR LIFE

In Jesus—as His ambassador, brother, and friend—I
have been commissioned to make disciples of people in
every nation, teaching them to abide by the Word in
every area of life. Jesus is always with me. He has given
me His word that He will never leave me nor forsake
me, even to the end of the age.

father got a phone call that his son had been arrested and was on his way to jail. A friend said to the man, "So, that son of yours is in trouble again."

"I'm afraid he is," said the father.

"Ah!" said the other man, "I know it is not the first time by any means. I know all you've tried to do for him in the past. But I gather the offense is worse than ever this time. Do you know what I would do if he were my son? I'd put him out the door, shut it, and then turn the key once and for all."

"Yes," said the father, "do you know that if he were a son of yours I would do exactly the same thing. But, you see, he is *my* son, and I will not do that."

God the Father has chosen you as His son/daughter, and He refuses to give up on you. He will do whatever it takes to show you His love.

This is how God showed his love among
us: He sent his one and only Son into
the world that we might live through him.
This is love: not that we loved God,
but that he loved us and sent his Son
as an atoning sacrifice for our sins.

1 JOHN 4:9–10

DECLARATION FOR YOUR LIFE

*God showed His own love for me by sending Jesus into
the world so that I might live through Him. This is
love in its purest form—not that I instigated this love
relationship I now enjoy with the Father, but He loved
me so much that He sent Jesus to me. He did this in
order to make me His own son/daughter. Indeed, I am
forgiven of all sin and am now the very son/daughter
of almighty God!*

t had been the custom of a kindly doctor to go through his books from time to time, noting those who had not paid their bills. When he realized the debts remained because the patients could not pay, he put a red line through the debt and wrote by the side of it, "Forgiven, unable to pay."

After his death, his wife was looking through his books and saw all the marks and said to herself, *My husband was owed a lot of money. I could do with that money now.* She took the matter to the local court to sue the debtors for the money. The judge, however, looked at the doctor's account book and said, "No court in the world will give you a verdict against those people when your husband, with his own pen, has written, 'Forgiven, unable to pay.'"

That's the definition of grace: forgiven, unable to pay. Like the good doctor, God has marked through your sins with the blood of Jesus and declared your forgiveness.

Have mercy upon me, O God,

According to Your lovingkindess;

According to the multitude of Your
tender mercies,

Blot out my transgressions.

Wash me thoroughly from my iniquity,

And cleanse me from my sin.

PSALM 51:1–2 NKJV

DECLARATION FOR YOUR LIFE

My Father has flooded me with His mercy. He loves me with all of His heart and has forgiven all of my sins. He has blotted out every transgression that I have, or ever will, commit. He has thoroughly stripped sin of its power in my life. I am now clean and perfect in His eyes.

A GIVING ATTITUDE

other Teresa told of a man who had been beaten up and was picked up on the streets of Melbourne. He was an alcoholic who had been in that state for years, and the Sisters took him to their Home of Compassion.

From the way they touched him and the way they took care of him, suddenly it was clear to him that "God loves me!" He left the Home and never touched alcohol again. Instead, he went back to his family, his children, and his job.

Afterward, when he received his first salary check, he came to the Sisters and gave them the money, saying, "I want you to be for others the love of God, as you have been to me."

When you fully grasp the love of God for you, you can't help but spread it on to others!

[The righteous man] hath dispersed,
he hath given to the poor;
his righteousness endureth for ever;
his horn shall be exalted with honour.

PSALM 112:9 KJV

DECLARATION FOR YOUR LIFE

I am known as a just and righteous man/woman. I distribute gifts regularly to those in need, and the resulting righteousness endures forever. When bad news comes, I am not shaken. I know the One in whom my trust is set, and my victory in the end is absolutely certain.

s you see yourself in the context of God's plan and purpose, begin to place a higher value on your time. Realize that every moment of your day counts for eternity. It's important for you to take care of yourself—spirit, soul, and body—in order to fulfill the exciting things that God has given you to do. That includes taking time for rest and relaxation, enjoying your family and friends, and spending time in God's presence. As He directs you, be quick to obey. As you put God's principles to work in your life, His blessings of health, strength, peace, provision, and joy will begin to overtake you.

I beseech you therefore, brethren, by the mercies of God, that ye present your bodies a living sacrifice, holy, acceptable unto God, which is your reasonable service. And be not conformed to this world: but be ye transformed by the renewing of your mind, that ye may prove what is that good, and acceptable, and perfect, will of God.

ROMANS 12:1–2 KJV

DECLARATION FOR YOUR LIFE

In view of God's mercy, I dedicate my body as a living sacrifice, holy and well pleasing to Him. This is my spiritual worship. I follow the ways of the spirit as I am led by the Holy Spirit. I do not conform to the ways of the world, but I am transformed by the renewing of my mind so that I may demonstrate the good, acceptable, and perfect will of God.

od has called you personally to fulfill an amazing purpose that only you can fulfill. But at times, following that call can be risky, especially when it involves doing something new, different, or even just outside of your comfort zone.

Thank God that He promises to always be with you to strengthen you and enable you to do those things He asks you to do. As you step out in faith, He steps right along with you. He will more than equip you for everything He has planned for you, and as you trust in Him, you will be astounded at all you and He will accomplish—together.

I am your Creator. You were in my
care even before you were born.

ISAIAH 44:2 CEV

DECLARATION FOR YOUR LIFE

*I have been chosen by God to be His own son/daugh-
ter. He actually picked me to be a part of His family.
He has recreated me in righteousness and helps me in
every area of my life. He proclaims His blessing on all
that I have and prospers all that I set my hand to do.*

A Flourishing Tree

s you seek God through His written Word and through prayer and fellowship, change happens. You may not even notice the difference at first. You will find that you have more patience, more joy, more self-control, and many other godly characteristics. Not only will you experience a spiritual transformation, but a natural one, as well. God will help you develop your natural gifts and talents so that you will not only be blessed, but you will also be a blessing.

God is always working ahead of you to bring you into His blessings, to bring you the good things that He has already prepared for you. As you walk with Him, you will become like a green and flourishing tree.

A life devoted to things is a dead life,
a stump; a God-shaped life
is a flourishing tree.

PROVERBS 11:28 THE MESSAGE

DECLARATION FOR YOUR LIFE

I seek what is good and find goodwill. By my actions, I show that my trust is not in riches, but in the prosperity that only God can provide. By Him, I have abundance and thrive like a green leaf.

hen you look at the whole of God's creation, has *anything* been created without a plan and a purpose? The natural world provides thousands—yes, millions and perhaps billions—of examples of cause and effect, action and response, and behavior and consequence. It is only rational to conclude that God—who created everything in this universe and who established all of the natural laws to govern His universe—would include a purpose for your life that includes cause and effect, action and response, and behavior and consequence. Who you will become in this life and what you do upon this earth is up to you—but God's plan for you was set in motion long ago. You were chosen before the foundation of the world—because of His great love for you.

Long before he laid down earth's
foundations, he had us in mind, had
settled on us as the focus of his love,
to be made whole and holy by his love.

EPHESIANS 1:4 THE MESSAGE

DECLARATION FOR YOUR LIFE

God chose me, in Jesus, before the creation of the world, to be holy and blameless in His sight. In His great love for me, He predestined me to be adopted as His son/daughter, through Jesus, in accordance with the good pleasure of His will.

enneth McAll, in his days as a missionary doctor in China, was once walking toward a desert village. He had already had one narrow escape when arrested and tried by the invading Japanese. As he walked, a man joined him and asked him to change direction and go to a different village. He turned and accompanied the man to their destination. When they arrived, the villagers were delighted and they needed plenty of help. "But why did you change direction?" they asked. "You were walking toward a village that is occupied by the Japanese." They said they had watched him walking in the desert but had seen no man stop and talk to him. When Kenneth looked around, there was no trace of the man. It was then that he realized his guide had spoken to him in English—something no one else in that region spoke.

God will guide your steps as you trust in Him.

[The Lord says], "I will instruct you and
teach you in the way you should go;
I will guide you with My eye."

PSALM 32:8 NKJV

DECLARATION FOR YOUR LIFE

*It is the God of all the universe, my own heavenly
Father, who counsels and watches over me with a
relentless eye.*

Building Your Character

ne area in which God always challenges us to grow and change is in our character. The Bible tells us that God is at work in every believer's life to conform that person into the character likeness of Christ Jesus. (Romans 8:29.)

God wants you to pay attention to the way that you are living your life and to allow yourself to be transformed into His image. Everyone can always be more loving. Everyone can always have greater joy, be more at peace, have greater patience, show more kindness, reflect more goodness, walk in greater faithfulness. They can express themselves with greater gentleness and manifest more self-control. No matter how mature you are, God's will for you is that you would grow more and more into His image and likeness.

Don't lose a minute in building on what you've been given, complementing your basic faith with good character, spiritual understanding, alert discipline, passionate patience, reverent wonder, warm friendliness, and generous love, each dimension fitting into and developing the others.

2 PETER 1:5-7 THE MESSAGE

DECLARATION FOR YOUR LIFE

I make every effort to add the goodness of God to my faith; and to goodness, knowledge; and to knowledge, self-control; and to self-control, perseverance; and to perseverance, godliness; and to godliness, brotherly kindness; and to brotherly kindness, love. By keeping all of these qualities in increasing measure, I remain effective and productive in my knowledge of Jesus.

GOD'S GOOD GIFTS

ig Ziglar tells the story of how one day he was trying to assemble a tricycle he had just bought for his then four-year-old son, Tom. Ziglar became more exasperated by the minute because the proverbial bolt A would not fit into proverbial nut B. He was about to give up when Tom, who was looking on, suddenly blurted, "I sure do love you, Dad!" Needless to say, Ziglar finished putting together that tricycle!

God can't wait to bring good things into your life. Just as a good father gives good gifts to his children, no matter what it takes, God has wonderful things in store for you!

I would have lost heart, unless I had believed
That I would see the goodness of the Lord
In the land of the living.

PSALM 27:13 NKJV

DECLARATION FOR YOUR LIFE

I remain steadfast and confident in the fact that I will
see the goodness of God in my life!

n Ephesians 1:3–4, the apostle Paul wrote, "How blessed is God! And what a blessing he is! He's the Father of our Master, Jesus Christ, and takes us to the high places of blessing in him. Long before he laid the earth's foundations, he had us in mind, had settled on us as the focus of his love, to be made whole and holy by his love" (THE MESSAGE). Notice that Paul did not say that God is *going* to bless us with spiritual blessings once we are in heaven, or even once we fulfill certain duties, roles, or commands that He has asked us to fulfill. Paul wrote that Jesus Christ *already* has made all of these blessings available to us. They are blessings that are already laid up in God's storehouse for us to claim.

You cannot have a need that takes God by surprise. You cannot have a need that is beyond the supply that has already been provided by your heavenly Father and made available to you by Christ Jesus!

Blessed be the God and Father of our Lord Jesus Christ, who hath blessed us with all spiritual blessings in heavenly places in Christ: According as he hath chosen us in him before the foundation of the world, that we should be holy and without blame before him.

EPHESIANS 1:3–4 KJV

DECLARATION FOR YOUR LIFE

I give all praise, honor, and glory to my God, the Father of my Lord Jesus, for He has blessed me with every spiritual blessing in Christ. He chose me, in Jesus, before the creation of the world, to be holy and blameless in His sight.

ohn White and his wife were missionaries in Malaysia. One day they were praying for a two-year-old child whose body was completely covered with raw, weeping eczema sores. She ran around the room restlessly so that her parents had to catch her to bring her, struggling, over to John and his wife.

They began to pray and extended their hands to lay them on her. The instant their hands touched the girl, she fell into a profound and relaxed slumber in her mother's arms. John said, "I shall never forget our sense of exhilaration and excitement as the weeping areas began to dry up, their borders shrinking visibly before our eyes like the shores of lakes in times of drought." Soon the girl was completely healed.

God wants you to be healed and whole in every area of your life—including your physical body. Trust Him for your healing today.

Beloved, I pray that you may prosper
in all things and be in health,
just as your soul prospers.

3 John 2 NKJV

Declaration for Your Life

*I know the heart of my Father—that He is a good
Father and wishes above all things that I prosper and
remain healthy, even as my soul prospers.*

round 1830, Crowfoot was born into the Bear Ghost family of Blackfoot Indians. While still a teenager, he won distinction for his bravery and scouting ability. He was soon the great chief of the Blackfoot confederacy of Indian nations in southern Alberta, Canada. In 1884, authorities from the Canadian Pacific Railway sought his permission to take the Atlantic to the Pacific railway line through the territory of his people from Medicine Hat to Alberta. During the negotiations, Canadian Pacific Railway agreed to give Crowfoot, in return, a lifetime rail pass. Crowfoot had a leather case made for the pass. He carried the pass with him, around his neck, wherever he went. However, there is no record of Crowfoot ever using the pass to travel anywhere on Canadian Pacific Railways.

God has given you His promises in His Word. But you must activate those promises in order for them to have an effect in your life. Don't just allow those promises to stay bound in leather, unused. Begin to speak them over your circumstances and watch God begin to work in your life.

Whatever God has promised gets stamped with the Yes of Jesus. In him, this is what we preach and pray, the great Amen, God's Yes and our Yes together, gloriously evident.

2 CORINTHIANS 1:20 THE MESSAGE

DECLARATION FOR YOUR LIFE

My heavenly Father is faithful to His every word. No matter how many promises He has made, in Jesus, He makes good on every one. I have God's Word; therefore, I have God's will. Every time I pray in line with His Word, the answer is guaranteed.

od gave you specific talents and abilities to use in fulfilling His plan and purposes for the ages. He made you to bring glory to Himself. He made you to have fellowship with Him and to be in a close, intimate relationship with Him.

There is no higher purpose than for a person to be a close personal friend of God and to use the talents that God has given him to the best of his ability all the days of his life. It is to this life that you are called. It is for this purpose that the Holy Spirit helps and guides you on a daily basis. It is for this reason that you have been brought into God's kingdom as His very special and beloved child.

Everything that goes into a life of pleasing
God has been miraculously given to us by
getting to know, personally and intimately,
the One who invited us to God.

2 PETER 1:3 THE MESSAGE

DECLARATION FOR YOUR LIFE

*As a born-again son/daughter of God: I have been
given all things that pertain unto life and godliness; I
have a deep and personal knowledge of Him who has
called me; I have entered into His own glory and goodness; and all of His great and precious promises are
applied to me.*

Put God First

uring the Great Depression, two families shared a house in Pennsylvania. One family occupied the upper floor, and the other family lived on the lower. The family which lived downstairs was always inviting people to share what they had. When there was an opportunity for them to give, they always seemed to have enough. The family on the upper floor, however, scoffed at the way the downstairs family lived. They stored all extras in a locker in the pantry. They gave nothing away. It was not until they found that rats had gotten into their pantry that they were sad about what they had done. Interestingly, the rats had not disturbed the downstairs pantry!

When we put God's kingdom first, God will bless us, and the blessing will be double because of the joy that it brings.

But seek ye first the kingdom of God,
and his righteousness; and all these
things shall be added unto you.

MATTHEW 6:33 KJV

DECLARATION FOR YOUR LIFE

My first thought in all things is the advancement of the kingdom and God's way of being and doing things. With this mindset and spiritual stronghold, all of my physical and material needs will shower into my life in a flood of abundance.

hen you come to the Lord to have Him meet your needs, come to Him with a heart open to receive all that He gives to you. Come with a desire to just sit for a while in the close presence of the Lord. Come with a willingness to be held tenderly in His everlasting arms. Allow yourself to relax in His presence.

If a sin comes to your mind, confess it to Him and receive His forgiveness. If a thought comes to your mind, express it to Him. If a word of praise fills your heart, voice it softly as if whispering it into His ear. Allow your time with Him to bring Him pleasure and cause you to experience the gentle warmth of God's Holy Spirit as it flows around you, in you, and through you.

Ask, and it shall be given you; seek, and
ye shall find; knock, and it shall be opened
unto you: For every one that asketh
receiveth; and he that seeketh findeth; and
to him that knocketh it shall be opened.

MATTHEW 7:7–8 KJV

DECLARATION FOR YOUR LIFE

*I will ask and keep on asking until I have received
what I am asking for. I will seek and keep on seeking
until I have found what I am looking for. I will knock
and keep on knocking until the door is opened unto
me. I know of a certainty that when I ask, I will receive;
when I seek, I will find; and when I knock, the door
will be opened to me.*

t is amazing the number of books that continue to be published . . . on the subject of self-esteem. The only conclusion that can be drawn is that so much self-esteem material continues to be produced because so many people are struggling with such a poor self-image. The reason for this poor self-image ultimately is that people do not see themselves as being valuable, worthy, or acceptable to God.

When a person knows he is of extreme importance to God, and God loves him, values him, and desires to be in close relationship with him, that person has confidence and a strong self-image.

Allow the wisdom of God to lead you to see yourself as God sees you—as someone whom He is delighted to spend time with and who is more than valuable in His eyes. Your steps are ordered by Him. He loves you so much that He has planned out your steps so that you can fulfill your destiny—a wonderful, abundant life.

The steps of a good man are ordered by
the Lord: and he delighteth in his way.

PSALM 37:23 KJV

DECLARATION FOR YOUR LIFE

*My Father is overjoyed to spend His time with me. He
rejoices as we walk this life together and He sees to it
that all of my steps stand firm.*

PAID IN FULL

igel is a young man who lives in Britain. On one occasion, he went to the United States. He had very little money for the trip. One day he was driving a borrowed car and went through a stop sign. Of course, the police were there waiting for him! Nigel pleaded with the man in blue, saying that he was a tourist and did not have a lot of money. But the policeman would hear none of his excuses and handed him a ticket.

The next day, when Nigel arrived home, there was a letter waiting for him. In it was a note from the policeman and a check for the amount of the fine.

Even if you sin, God has made provision for your forgiveness. Jesus Christ has already paid the penalty for your sin—so that you can be restored in full into a right relationship with the Father God.

If anyone should sin, we have an Advocate (One Who will intercede for us) with the Father—[it is] Jesus Christ [the all] righteous [upright, just, Who conforms to the Father's will in every purpose, thought, and action]. And He [that same Jesus Himself] is the propitiation (the atoning sacrifice) for our sins, and not for ours alone but also for [the sins of] the whole world.

1 JOHN 2:1–2 AMP

DECLARATION FOR YOUR LIFE

If I do sin, I have One who speaks to God the Father in my defense: my Lord and Savior, Jesus Christ the righteous. He is the propitiation (the go-between; the One who makes amends) for my sins, and not for mine only, but also for the sins of the whole world.

A GREAT INHERITANCE

homeless man in Pennsylvania once said:

"I got off at the Pittsburgh depot one day as a tramp, and for a year I begged on the street for a living. One day I touched a man on the shoulder and said, 'Mister, please give me a dime.' As soon as I saw his face I recognized my old father. 'Father, don't you know me?' I asked. Throwing his arms around me, he cried, 'I have found you. I have found you! All that I have is yours.'"

The homeless man, who became a Christian, went on to say, "Think of it, that I, a tramp, stood begging my father for ten cents when for eighteen years, he had been looking for me, to give me all he was worth."

God is on the search for you, His chosen child, to give you, not a dime, but everything that He has. As His child, you share in the same inheritance as Jesus!

For as many as are led by the Spirit
of God, they are the sons of God.
The Spirit itself beareth witness with
our spirit, that we are the children
of God: And if children, then heirs;
heirs of God, and joint-heirs with Christ....

ROMANS 8:14, 16–17 KJV

DECLARATION FOR YOUR LIFE

*By living under the guidance of the Holy Spirit, I
demonstrate the fact that I am a son/daughter of God.
As God's own son/daughter, I share in the same inheritance that Jesus does!*

f you are not fully aware today of the unique talents and gifts that God has given to you—as His child—and that have been present in you from your birth, ask God to reveal those gifts to you.

Once God reveals your unique talents, ask Him to help you develop them. Be sensitive to ways in which you might receive further training in your areas of talent. As you develop your talents, ask God to reveal ways in which you can use them for His glory. Don't wait until you are an expert. Part of the way to become an expert is to start using your talents for God's purposes. In this way, you, God's dearly beloved child, can give Him glory through your life.

And it was only right that God—
who made everything and for whom
everything was made—should bring
his many children into glory.

HEBREWS 2:10 NLT

DECLARATION FOR YOUR LIFE

*What a wonder it is that I have become the very
son/daughter of the Creator of the universe! I have been
created for His glory.*

od desires that we develop in our talents, aptitudes, and ministry gifts every day of our lives—just as Jesus did. We should never stop practicing or stop learning, no matter how experienced or skilled we may become. The truly great concert pianists still practice scales on a routine basis. Top athletes still work out and practice "basic drills" during training camps and warm-up sessions, no matter how many years they've been in the professional ranks.

God will not lead you to "become" something without aiding you to become the "best" you can possibly be in that area. He will not give you a talent and then fail to give you opportunities for discovering, using, developing, practicing, and perfecting it. As you practice being like Jesus, maintaining a mind and an attitude like His, your talents will be developed to their fullest potential!

Since Jesus went through everything
you're going through and more,
learn to think like him.

1 PETER 4:1 THE MESSAGE

DECLARATION FOR YOUR LIFE

I am armed with the mind and attitude of Christ.

Set Free!

I t is told that once, in the days before the ending of slavery, Abraham Lincoln bought a slave girl with the sole purpose of giving her, her freedom. She did not realize why he was buying her; she thought it was simply another transaction in which she was involved as a "thing." He paid the price for her and then handed her, her papers of freedom. She did not even understand. "You are free," he said to her gently.

"Free?" she said. "Can I go wherever I want to go now?"

"Indeed you can," he replied.

"Then," she said, "if I am free to go anywhere, I will stay with you and serve you until I die."

Jesus has set you free from the curse of the Law. You are now free to serve God as His son/daughter and receive all of the promises that go along with that privilege.

When the fulness of the time was come,
God sent forth his Son, made of a woman,
made under the law, to redeem them
that were under the law, that we might
receive the adoption of sons.

GALATIANS 4:4–5 KJV

DECLARATION FOR YOUR LIFE

*Jesus redeemed me from the curse of the Law so that I
could claim full rights as a son/daughter of God.
I now have a right to every promise that God has ever
made to His people.*

osario is a woman from Peru. She was a terrorist, a brute of a woman who was an expert in several martial arts. In her terrorist activities, she had killed twelve policemen. She had heard a little of the story of Jesus and was incensed at the Christian message. When she heard that Luis Palau was conducting a Christian meeting in Lima, she set out to kill Palau.

She made her way into the stadium where Palau was speaking. As she sat there trying to work out how she was going to get close to the speaker, she began to listen to the message. Instead of shooting Palau, she met Jesus.

Ten years later, Luis Palau met Rosario for the first time. During those years, she had assisted in planting five churches and had founded an orphanage that houses over 1,000 children.

With Jesus inside of you, think of the souls you could bring to God, the people you could touch, the amazing destiny you could fulfill. The hand of the Lord is upon you to bring people back to Him!

The hand of the Lord was with them,
and a great number believed
and turned to the Lord.

ACTS 11:21 NKJV

DECLARATION FOR YOUR LIFE

The presence of the Lord is continually with me in power, making me an effective soul winner.

No Longer a Servant, but a Friend

 esus challenged His disciples to be perfect—to be made whole and complete—to lay down their old lives and pick up the new lives He would give them.

No friend will ever challenge you to the heights that Jesus challenges you. Whatever Jesus commands you to do, He will enable you to do. He is a Friend who not only tells you what to do, but He is a Friend who will walk through life with you every step of the way, guiding you and empowering you to live out the life that He calls you to live.

You are no longer a stranger to Jesus; you are His friend! You are a member of God's precious family, chosen to live the life that He has called you to live.

[Jesus said], "You are My friends if you do whatever I command you. No longer do I call you servants, for a servant does not know what his master is doing; but I have called you friends, for all things that I heard from My Father I have made known to you."

JOHN 15:14–15 NKJV

DECLARATION FOR YOUR LIFE

I am Jesus' close friend and I continually do what He has commanded me to do. He does not call me a servant, for a servant does not know his master's business. To the contrary, He calls me His close friend and continually reveals to me His will and purpose—even all that He knows.

eople need other people. We each need relationships with others who are comparable to us—in values, desires, goals, beliefs, and to a degree, personality—so that we might receive help from them and help them in return. We need other people in order to grow into the fullness of our own potential and in order that we might experience a mutual giving and receiving of love and kindness.

A real friend is one who sticks closer than a brother (see Proverbs 18:24). He will be there through thick and thin—in good times and bad. He will provide strength so that you do not crumble in the face of evil or calamity. He remains rock-solid and steadfast in times of trauma. The truest Friend you will ever have is Jesus. He chose you and laid down His very life to save you and provide you with His abundant life.

Jesus Christ laid down his life for us.
And we ought to lay down
our lives for our brothers.

1 JOHN 3:16

DECLARATION FOR YOUR LIFE

This is how I know what love is: Jesus Christ laid down His life for me. In light of this, I will lay down my life for my brothers and sisters in the Lord. If I see someone in need, and I have the means to help them, I will do so.

aul wrote to the Philippian church: "I can do all things through Christ who strengthens me" (Philippians 4:13 NKJV). Does that mean that Paul could literally do all things? Was he talented in every area of life? No. Paul was the first to admit his weaknesses and failures. But Paul could do *all things through Christ who strengthened him.* Paul could do whatever the Lord empowered and enabled him to do. He was completely reliant upon God to do His work in him and through him.

You, too, can do whatever He leads you to do if you trust in Him to give you the ability and the power to do it. Nothing is beyond the realm of possibility if you trust God to help you fulfill His plan for your life. When God gives you a destination point, He will give you the road on which to travel in order to reach that destination.

Whatever I have, wherever I am, I can make it through anything in the One who makes me who I am.

PHILIPPIANS 4:13 THE MESSAGE

DECLARATION FOR YOUR LIFE

I can do all things through the power of Christ that is within me. With His anointing, there isn't a single circumstance that can hold me down! I am self-sufficient in His sufficiency.

GOD'S WORKMANSHIP

 s Jesus the Lord of everything or only of some things? Is He Lord over time, situations, the material universe, and all circumstances? Indeed, He is! Is He Lord over your life? That is a question that only you can answer. The truth, however, is that if you have made Jesus the Lord of your life, and He is the rightful King of all kings and Lord of all lords, then there isn't a situation, circumstance, or problem over which Jesus does not have absolute control and sovereignty. You are therefore His workmanship, and you have a great purpose in life—to do the good works that God sets before you. As you do these good works, God will make certain that all things come together for your good, in His timing and according to His chosen methods, if you will only trust Him completely to be the Lord of your life.

We are his workmanship, created in Christ
Jesus unto good works, which God hath
before ordained that we should walk in them.

EPHESIANS 2:10 KJV

DECLARATION FOR YOUR LIFE

*I am God's workmanship, recreated in Christ Jesus so
that I can have the ability to do the works that He has
foreordained that I should do. God has a plan for my
life, and He has set me on a prearranged path that is
leading me to my destiny in Jesus.*

LIVING IN PEACE

he Greek word for *peace* means "to bind together" something that has been broken or disjointed. This is a superb illustration for how alienated men and women—so often feeling empty and disconnected from each other and God—can find a way to unity and wholeness. God's peace comes to you when you are united by faith with God.

This Greek word also refers to a prevailing sense of quietness and rest in a person's heart and emotions—of being unperturbed and unruffled. Peace is synonymous with being tranquil, serene, untroubled, and calm.

One way that God wants to bless you, His chosen child, is with His peace—peace both with God and with other people.

Each one of you is part of the body
of Christ, and you were chosen
to live together in peace.

COLOSSIANS 3:15 CEV

DECLARATION FOR YOUR LIFE

*I allow the peace of Christ to rule in my heart. I will
never forget that as a member of the body of Christ I
am called to be at peace.*

Do Your Best

n Colossians 3:23, the apostle Paul
wrote: "Whatever you do, do it heartily,
as to the Lord and not to men" (NKJV).

When you receive the new nature, you
receive a new calling, and God asks you to do His
work. Paul defined this new work to be "whatever you
do." Because we are servants of God and are being
renewed into His image, everything we do is to be
considered part of our service to God. He makes no
distinction between what is spiritual and what is secular.
He chooses us to do what is best suited for us in order
to serve His kingdom—in whatever ways we can.

All of us who know the Lord—homemakers,
bankers, mechanics, assembly-line workers, construc-
tion workers—are involved in God's work, when we
are doing what He has asked us to do. We are all a
part of His design and plan for our generation. It takes
just as much dependency on the Holy Spirit to do any
of these jobs well as it does to preach a sermon or
sing in the choir. In some cases, it takes much more!

God has chosen you to do a specific job in His
kingdom, so do it with all of your might.

Do your best. Work from the heart for your real Master, for God, confident that you'll get paid in full when you come into your inheritance. Keep in mind always that the ultimate Master you're serving is Christ.

COLOSSIANS 3:22–24
THE MESSAGE

DECLARATION FOR YOUR LIFE

Whatever God asks me to do, I will work at with all of my heart. I know that I am working for the Lord. I know that the Lord is always watching over me carefully, and He longs to grant me a specific inheritance as a reward for honoring Him. In all of my work, I will remember that it is Jesus Himself whom I am serving.

Grow Up in the Word

hen you grow up in the Word of God and become a maturing Christian, you will be able to stand rock solid in Him and in His wisdom. The good news about God's wisdom is this: Every person *can* become wise. That isn't true for fame, fortune, or education. Not all people have the intellectual ability to earn college degrees. Not all people have the talents or attributes that contribute to fame. Not all people have the skills and opportunities necessary for acquiring wealth.

But every person can reverence God, can receive Jesus Christ as Savior, and can submit his or her life to God on a daily basis. *Every* person—including *you*—can become wise.

We should no longer be children, tossed to
and fro and carried about with every wind
of doctrine, by the trickery of men, in the
cunning craftiness of deceitful plotting, but,
speaking the truth in love, may grow up in
all things into Him who is the head—Christ.

EPHESIANS 4:14–15 NKJV

DECLARATION FOR YOUR LIFE

*I am no longer like an infant, tossed back and forth by
every wind of doctrine that comes into my life. I will
not fall as prey to the cunning craftiness of deceitful
men who twist the Word of God to their own ends (to
fit their traditions, fill their pocketbooks, etc.). By
continually speaking the truth in love, I will, in all
things, grow up into a mature man/woman in Christ,
who is the executive Lord of my life.*

TRUST YOURSELF TO GOD'S CARE

avid did not immediately go from being a favorite person in the king's court to becoming king. The Lord allowed David to be in exile for more than a decade, all the while refining certain leadership skills in him. While in exile, David wrote many of the psalms that we have in our Bibles today. In exile, David learned to trust God in all circumstances, regardless of his personal feelings. Those years of being on the run from Saul, often fearful for his very life, were years that God worked for David's good, years in which the Lord used the circumstances to refine certain competencies in David—to make him an excellent statesman and military commander, as well as a compassionate leader and provider for his people.

When you trust yourself in the Lord's care, and know that He has called you to a greater destiny than what your circumstances seem to indicate, He is able to use those circumstances to your advantage. He is *well* able to fulfill the destiny that He has for you—a tremendous inheritance He has chosen especially for you.

Now I'm turning you over to God, our
marvelous God whose gracious Word can
make you into what he wants you to be
and give you everything you could possibly
need in this community of holy friends.

ACTS 20:32 THE MESSAGE

DECLARATION FOR YOUR LIFE

*I am entrusted to God and the Word of His grace. He
is well able to build me up, establish me, and fulfill my
part of His tremendous inheritance among my brothers and sisters in Christ.*

You Are Worthy!

e do not acquire feelings of self-worth by standing in front of a mirror and repeating to ourselves, "I am worthy. I am worthy. I am worthy." We acquire feelings of self-worth when we stand in front of the cross and come to the realization of the greatest truth of all time: "I am worthy because God says I am worthy. I am worthy because Jesus died in my place, for my sins, so that I might live in eternity with God."

God purposed to send Jesus to give you this eternal life. He chose you from the foundation of the world, to provide for you the new birth through the blood of Jesus and set you free from every bondage you might experience. You are the most important of all things He has made. Tell yourself *that* the next time you look in the mirror!

God decided to give us life through the word of truth so we might be the most important of all the things he made.

JAMES 1:18 NCV

DECLARATION FOR YOUR LIFE

Out of the purpose of His own heart, God chose to give me the new birth through the Word of Truth, making me a new creation in Christ Jesus my Lord.

CHOSEN BY GOD

esus has called us and chosen us to be His disciples in the earth. First Peter 2:9 (NKJV) tells us that "you are a *chosen* generation, a royal priesthood . . . His own special people" (emphasis added). Despite this, each of us will always have plenty of room for growth, and that's part of God's design for us. We also will never be fully adequate in and of ourselves, but with His Spirit residing in us, we will be more than adequate for any task that He sets before us. God is the Author and the Finisher of our lives—not only of our faith, but also of all aspects of the potential He has built into us!

Don't ever lock yourself into saying, "I can't, I can't, I can't," when you feel less than fully competent. Instead, say, "By the grace of God and with the help of God's Spirit, which lives in me, I *can!*"

You are the ones chosen by God, chosen
for the high calling of priestly work, chosen
to be a holy people, God's instruments to
do his work and speak out for him, to tell
others of the night-and-day difference he
made for you—from nothing to something,
from rejected to accepted.

1 Peter 2:9-10 The Message

Declaration for Your Life

*I have been specifically chosen by God to be a royal
priest in His household—a citizen of a holy nation—
a son/daughter of God, who is of God, and in every
way belonging to Him. I have been snatched out of
darkness and translated into His wonderful light. I
give Him praise, honor, and glory for what He has
done for me.*

early thirty years ago, Maurice Wright, a farmer, bought a large painting from a neighboring farmer for a couple of dollars and hung it in his barn. After collecting cobwebs for several years, the painting was noticed by the farmer's tax accountant. Wondering what it might be worth, he took a color photograph of it and sent the photo to Christie's, the well-known London auction firm. Subsequently, he learned that the painting might be the work of Thomas Daniell, a highly acclaimed nineteenth-century artist.

The painting turned out to be an 1808 Daniell. Art critics had been aware of its existence, but it had come to be known as the "Lost Daniell," its whereabouts having been a mystery for over a century. Wright sold the painting at an auction—for more than $90,000!

The treasure of the Gospel resides in you, an earthen vessel. And it is even more valuable than the painting hanging in the barn.

But we have this treasure in earthen
vessels, that the excellency of the power
may be of God, and not of us.

2 CORINTHIANS 4:7 KJV

DECLARATION FOR YOUR LIFE

*In Christ, I have insight and all ability to understand
His glory in this earth. I have this treasure as in a jar
of clay to show that the all-surpassing power that
flows in and through me is from God and not my own.*

GOD'S GREATEST GIFT

ne of God's greatest gifts is His grace
and forgiveness, available to us
through Jesus Christ. If God has
forgiven you, forgive others, forgive yourself, and then
open yourself up to the good opportunities that God
has for you. You are never required by God to live
with guilt, shame, or regret. Accept that your past
mistakes have happened, but quickly acknowledge the
greater truth that your past mistakes—now forgiven by
God—do not need to impact the decisions or choices
you will make in the future.

Let us have confidence, then, and approach
God's throne, where there is grace.
There we will receive mercy and find
grace to help us just when we need it.

HEBREWS 4:16 TEV

DECLARATION FOR YOUR LIFE

*In Jesus, the way has been opened for me to freely
receive God's help in any and every circumstance I find
myself in. It doesn't matter if it is my fault or not, for
by His grace (unmerited, undeserved favor) He has
given me His Word that He will help me and put me
back on my feet.*

BRIGHT AND BEAUTIFUL

he best picture of what a Spirit-filled person looks like is Jesus Christ. His life was characterized by love, joy, peace, patience, goodness, gentleness, and self-control, in the midst of a world characterized by just the opposite of those things. He was certainly not weak. He stood up to His detractors and opponents when it was appropriate. But He knew when to keep silent, as well. He had the courage and the wit to take on the intellectuals of His day. He spoke with authority—He was secure in Himself and in the destiny to which He knew the Father had called Him. There was nothing pretentious or intimidating about Him. At the end of His life, He tackled the toughest opponent of all—death. And He won!

The Bible says that "those who receive the abundance of grace and of the gift of righteousness will reign in life through the One, Jesus Christ" (Romans 5:17 NASB). Thank God that through the Holy Spirit, you can live like Jesus lived, victorious in the destiny to which God has called you!

Our lives gradually [become] brighter
and more beautiful as God enters
our lives and we become like him.

2 CORINTHIANS 3:18 THE MESSAGE

DECLARATION FOR YOUR LIFE

*I am continually being transformed into the likeness of
Him with ever-increasing glory, which comes from the
Lord, who is the Spirit and who dwells with me.*

od's promises are sure—they will most certainly be fulfilled!

When we approach and declare the promises of God in the Bible, we do so not on the basis of our own merits, anything we have done ourselves, but on the basis that our position is in Christ. We can declare the promises as true for us because of what Jesus has done for us, what God has said He would do for us, and what the Holy Spirit is available to do in us, through us, and for us. Our access to the reality of God's promises is not based on anything that we are or have done, but it is based on who God is, what Jesus Christ has done, and what the Holy Spirit desires to do.

God has a clear-cut plan for your life—things that He has promised to fulfill. Keep that plan ever before you, and claim His promises as true, not because of your own strength or goodness, but because of who He is in your life!

[The Lord's] compassions fail not.
They are new every morning:
great is thy faithfulness.

LAMENTATIONS 3:22–23 KJV

DECLARATION FOR YOUR LIFE

God's compassion for me never fails. He renews His love and blessings for me every morning and is faithful to fulfill the plan He has for my life.

VICTORY IN JESUS

n Sunday evening, June 18, 1815, a few kilometers south of Brussels in Belgium, the Battle of Waterloo was over. The British had won. Wellington needed to send news of his victory back to England. His men set up a series of line-to-sight communication stations and a coded message was sent. But only the first part of the message got through. Halfway through sending the message, the fog set in, and the signalers could not see each other. All the English received was the terrible news: "Wellington defeated…" However, later the fog lifted and the whole message could get through: "Wellington defeated Napoleon at Waterloo."

The message of the Gospel is clear to you today: Victory has been secured through the Lord Jesus Christ!

Thanks be to God, which giveth us the
victory through our Lord Jesus Christ.
Therefore, my beloved brethren, be ye
stedfast, unmoveable, always abounding
in the work of the Lord.

1 Corinthians
15:57–58 KJV

Declaration for Your Life

*Thanks be to God I have the victory over sin and death
through Jesus Christ my Lord. Therefore, I shall let
nothing move me to fear. I always give myself fully to
the work of the Lord, because I know of a certainty that
my labor in Him is not in vain.*

You're Worth It!

 our heavenly Father chose you and paid a very high price to redeem you to Himself—the life of His own Son, Jesus. And now your heavenly Father has offered you the most amazing gift that you could ever receive—the gift of His Son, full forgiveness of your sins through your belief in His Son, and the gift of His Holy Spirit living on the inside of you. If God was willing to pay such a price to give you these things, He is not going to withhold from you anything that will enable you or assist you in the task to which He has now called you: taking Jesus into the world in which you live and work.

God desires for you to display your relationship with Jesus in every facet of your life, and He will grant every request that you make that furthers the witness of Christ Jesus in you and through you this day.

God paid a great price for you.

1 Corinthians 6:20 CEV

DECLARATION FOR YOUR LIFE

I am not my own person; I am God's. He has paid a tremendous price for me.

alatians 5:25 instructs, "If we live in the Spirit, let us also walk in the Spirit" (KJV). Just as unconditional love shines brightest in the midst of our differences, so the fruit of the Spirit, the very essence of the image and character of Jesus, demonstrates its divine source when circumstances or relationships take a turn for the worse. The reason is, the fruit of the Spirit is just that: *fruit produced by the Spirit*. It is not fragile. It is not subject to change. Its root is deeply embedded in the person of Jesus Christ, in His image and likeness.

When you abide in Him and allow Him to live His life through you, the result is character that endures—and overcomes—the challenges of life!

Since this is the kind of life we have chosen,
the life of the Spirit, let us make sure that we
do not just hold it as an idea in our heads or
a sentiment in our hearts, but work out its
implications in every detail of our lives.

GALATIANS 5:25 THE MESSAGE

DECLARATION FOR YOUR LIFE

*I now live by my recreated spirit, as led by the Holy
Spirit. Therefore, as I live by my spirit, my conduct will
reflect what my spirit desires.*

It sounded like a good idea at the time. When Indonesian President Susilo Bambang Yudhoyono wanted to emphasize his desire to help cut through bureaucracy, he decided to make his cell phone number available to the public.

His political savvy was short-circuited, however, when he quickly received thousands of text messages. The increased volume overloaded his phone just one day after he had invited citizens to contact him directly.

God has a much simpler system for cutting through bureaucracy, one that doesn't fail or require assistance from a tech team! Call on the Lord. He has chosen you to be a part of His royal family, and He is always available to you.

Ye are a chosen generation, a royal
priesthood, an holy nation, a peculiar people;
that ye should shew forth the praises
of him who hath called you out of
darkness into his marvelous light.

DECLARATION FOR YOUR LIFE

I have been specifically chosen by God to be a royal
priest in His household—a citizen of a holy nation—
a son/daughter of God who is of God and in every way
belonging to Him. I have been snatched out of dark-
ness and translated into His wonderful light.

GOD WILL GUIDE YOU

 young man was discussing his love life—or rather, his lack of a love life—with his grandfather. He admitted to his grandfather that he hadn't been out on a date in several months. He finally gave a big sigh and said, "Gramps, I guess I'm just going to have to trust God to send me a wife."

His grandfather replied with a twinkle in his eye, "I suspect that God would be a lot more eager to help you out if He knew you had the nerve to ask the girl He sends you out on a date!"

Isaiah 58:11 says that "the Lord will guide you continually" (NLT). Many times God will reveal His plan for you, for meeting your needs or blessing His body, and that plan will include something specific that you must do. And most of the time, that action will ultimately be for your own benefit. Just as that young man had to do something, God may ask you to *do* something, as well. He asks you to use the gifts and talents He has given you, and in the process, He will meet every need in your life.

And the Lord shall guide you continually
and satisfy you in drought and in dry
places and make strong your bones. And
you shall be like a watered garden and like
a spring of water whose waters fail not.

ISAIAH 58:11 AMP

DECLARATION FOR YOUR LIFE

*The Lord guides me continually and satisfies my every
need even in a fruitless and sun-scorched land. He
strengthens my frame and makes me like a well-
watered garden—like a spring whose waters never fail.*

im was driving too fast late one night when he saw the flashing lights of a police car in his rearview mirror. As he pulled over and rolled down the window of his station wagon, he tried to dream up an excuse for his haste. But when the patrolman reached the car, he said nothing. Instead, he merely shined his flashlight on Jim's face, then on his seven-months-pregnant wife, then on their snoozing 18-month-old in his car seat, then on their three other children, who were also asleep, and finally on the two dogs in the very back of the car. Returning the beam of light to Jim's face, he then uttered the only words of the encounter.

"Son," he said, "you can't afford a ticket. Slow it down." And with that, he returned to his car and drove away.

Sometimes mercy triumphs over law! So it is for those of us who call on Jesus Christ.

So speak and so do as those who
will be judged by the law of liberty.

JAMES 2:12 NKJV

DECLARATION FOR YOUR LIFE

*I speak and act as one who will be judged under the
law of liberty, for I know that judgment without mercy
is given to those who are merciless. And, glory be to
God, I know that mercy triumphs over judgment!*

od wants us to respond to Him out of love and devotion. Romans 5:1 says, "Having been justified by faith, we have peace with God through our Lord Jesus Christ" (NASB). Our motivation in serving others and in fulfilling the destiny for which God has chosen us should be solely because we love God, not because we think we have to do certain good works to please Him.

When you love another person, you are quick to see what you can do to show that person how much you love him or her. That's far different from doing things for a person so that the other person might approve of you, like you, or love you. The same is true for your relationship with God. He already loves you, likes you, and approves of you. Nothing you can do will change that. There shouldn't be anything that you feel you have to do to win God's approval—you already have it.

Now the God of peace, that brought again
from the dead our Lord Jesus, that great
shepherd of the sheep, through the blood
of the everlasting covenant, make you
perfect in every good work to do his will,
working in you that which is wellpleasing in
his sight, through Jesus Christ; to whom
be glory for ever and ever. Amen.

HEBREWS 13:20–21 KJV

DECLARATION FOR YOUR LIFE

*My heavenly Father is the God of peace who brought
my Lord Jesus (my Shepherd and Master) back from
the dead. Through the blood of the eternal covenant,
He strengthens me and supplies me with everything
that is good.*

One young resident student had a marvelous effect on the children in his care at a local hospital. They responded to him with delight. The staff assigned a nurse to discover what the secret of this young resident was. It wasn't until the second week when she was on night duty that she learned what was going on. Every night on his last round, the student would kiss, hug, and tuck in every one of the children. It was in that act of compassion and sympathy that he made the contact—just as the compassion and sympathy of Jesus has reached out to us and charmed us in ways we could never have dreamed of.

Napoleon Bonaparte once said: "Alexander, Caesar, and Hannibel may have conquered the world, but they had no friends. Jesus founded His empire upon love, and at this hour, millions would die for Him. He has won the hearts of men, a task a conqueror cannot do."

Has the love of God won *your* heart today?

This is how God showed his love among us:
He sent his one and only Son into the
world that we might live through him.
This is love: not that we loved God,
but that he loved us and sent his Son
as an atoning sacrifice for our sins.

1 JOHN 4:9–10

DECLARATION FOR YOUR LIFE

God showed His own love for me by sending Jesus into the world so that I might live through Him. This is love in its purest form—not that I instigated this love relationship I now enjoy with the Father, but He loved me so much that He sent Jesus to me. He did this so that He could turn His wrath away from me and make me His own son/daughter. Indeed, I am forgiven of all sin and am now the very son/daughter of almighty God!

t is one thing to know what to do and another thing to do it. We must consciously and intentionally ask the Holy Spirit to guide us into wisdom and give us the courage, and most especially, the patience, to walk in it.

Proverbs 2:6 says that "the Lord gives wisdom, and from his mouth come knowledge and understanding." Part of this wisdom includes the "endurance factor"—the ability to look beyond present circumstances and endure with patience until the promised blessings arrive. You may continually find yourself in new situations, facing new circumstances. To walk wisely, to run the race with patience, you must consciously and intentionally ask the Lord daily to reveal His wisdom in every area of challenge, difficulty, or opportunity you face.

[We must] run with patience the particular
race that God has set before us.

HEBREWS 12:1 TLB

DECLARATION FOR YOUR LIFE

*I am resolved to run my race with patient endurance
and unwavering persistence.*

f there ever was a group who should have been able to live a consistent Christian life by simply doing their best, it was the apostles. Think of all their advantages. They had been trained by the Master Himself. They had seen lame men walk, blind men see, and the dead be raised to life. They had even performed miracles themselves!

Yet in their last encounter with the Savior, He let them know that they were still missing something: Jesus knew they were not yet ready for the task to which they had been called. They would need more than their own mere human spirits to carry them through. They would need more than sheer determination to fulfill the task and the purpose to which they had been called. They would need the Holy Spirit. Fortunately, Jesus promised: "You shall receive power when the Holy Spirit has come upon you" (Acts 1:8 NKJV). And that promise holds true for you today. When you receive the infilling of the Holy Spirit into your life, you will be able to fulfill the destiny for which God has chosen you.

[Jesus said], "When the Holy Spirit comes on you, you will be able to be my witnesses in Jerusalem, all over Judea and Samaria, even to the ends of the world."

ACTS 1:8 THE MESSAGE

DECLARATION FOR YOUR LIFE

As a result of my baptism in the Holy Spirit, and His indwelling of my spirit, I have received power (miraculous ability) and have become a living witness, demonstrating God's presence with me to my neighborhood, my city, my country, and the uttermost parts of the earth.

The Wisdom of God

e must choose to pursue wisdom. It's up to each of us to determine how we will walk through this life—and God asks us to give ourselves fully to His work, to walk in His wisdom and His ways. Wisdom is not something a person stumbles into or acquires automatically; rather, it must be sought out and pursued, just as it is with God's purposes and God's ways. God wants us to "throw ourselves into" seeking Him and His wisdom, in order to receive the blessings He promises.

The person who walks in God's wisdom is very aware of his life, how he affects the world, and how the world affects him. He seeks to know God's plan and purpose—not only for his own personal life, but also for every situation involving the people around him.

Wisdom is supreme; therefore get wisdom.
  Though it cost all you have,
    get understanding.

PROVERBS 4:7

DECLARATION FOR YOUR LIFE

Wisdom is the principle thing in my life. Therefore, I will get wisdom. And with all of my getting, I will get understanding. As I exalt wisdom in my life, she promotes me. When I embrace her, she brings me to honor. She places upon my head an ornament of grace. A crown of glory does she deliver to me. By wisdom, my days are prolonged upon the earth and I receive an abundance of everlasting rewards.

THE BENEFITS OF KNOWING GOD

ow do you get a great parking space at a New York Yankees baseball game? One man thought he had a way. He pulled his car into the VIP parking lot and casually told the attendant that he was a friend of George Steinbrenner, owner of the Yankees. Unfortunately for the imposter, the person attending the parking lot that day was George Steinbrenner himself, as he was doing some personal investigation of traffic problems at the stadium.

The surprised imposter looked at Steinbrenner and said, "Guess I've got the wrong lot." You can be sure that he did not park in the VIP lot that day—or ever!

The Owner knows his friends. God Himself has called you as one of His chosen ones, and because of your relationship with Him, you can exercise your benefits as a child of God.

[Jesus said], "Enter through the narrow gate. For wide is the gate and broad is the road that leads to destruction, and many enter through it. But small is the gate and narrow the road that leads to life, and only a few find it."

MATTHEW 7:13–14

DECLARATION FOR YOUR LIFE

I enter into God's blessings His way. I keep a distinct focus on that narrow gate that stands before me and do all that my Father says so that I may enter through it and obtain all of the blessings that come from the God-kind of life.

GOD IS LOVE

od is love, and He chooses to work through us and our human frailties, to make us more than conquerors in our lives. In the end, it is love—and especially the infinite, unconditional, forgiving love of God, our heavenly Father—that creates in us a feeling of value and worth. He chose us—He chose *you*—to be His child, and to be used for His glory.

If Jesus, God's Son, went to the cross for you, then surely you are worthy of His calling. If Christ died so that you might live with God forever in a heavenly home, then surely you have infinite value. If God created you, redeemed you, and desires to call you His child forever, then surely you are of great importance to Him.

The answer to feelings of unworthiness is love. An always-and-forever kind of love. A love that is not based on what you do, but upon who you are—a beloved child of almighty God.

Beloved, let us love one another, for love is of God; and everyone who loves is born of God and knows God.

1 JOHN 4:7 NKJV

DECLARATION FOR YOUR LIFE

I show my love for the body of Christ continually. All of my ability to love comes from God. As I am in Him, and He in me, His love pours forth from me in abundance. I love because I have been born of God and know God.

THE GOD OF HOPE

n 1997, the journal of the American Health Association reported on some remarkable research. According to the *Chicago Tribune*, Susan Everson of the Human Population Laboratory of the Public Health Institute in Berkeley, California, found that people who experienced high levels of despair had a 20 percent greater occurrence of atherosclerosis—the narrowing of their arteries—than did optimistic people. "This is the same magnitude of increased risk that one sees in comparing a pack-a-day smoker to a nonsmoker," said Everson. In other words, despair can be as bad for you as smoking a pack of cigarettes a day!

That is just one more reason why God has called us to choose hope and faith. The Christian life contributes to good health, for God gives us a legitimate basis for hope—an exciting, new life in the Spirit.

Now the God of hope fill you with all joy and peace in believing, that ye may abound in hope, through the power of the Holy Ghost. And I myself also am persuaded of you, my brethren, that ye also are full of goodness, filled with all knowledge, able also to admonish one another.

ROMANS 15:13–14 KJV

DECLARATION FOR YOUR LIFE

My heavenly Father, the God of all hope, fills me with all joy and peace as I believe in Him. I overflow with hope through the Holy Spirit who is within me. In Him, I am full of goodness, complete in knowledge, and well able to teach others the things that I know.

astor and author Tony Evans says: "One day I was in an airport, rushing to catch a plane. I was sweating and puffing when I looked to my right and saw a man walking half as fast as I was, but going faster. He was walking on a moving sidewalk.

"When we walk in the Spirit, He comes underneath us and bears us along. We're still walking, but we walk dependent on Him."[1]

When you follow the leading of the Holy Spirit, He comes underneath you and enables you to do what God has called you to do. Let nothing else move you but the Holy Spirit—but allow Him to move you into a greater calling than you have ever imagined.

For as many as are led by the Spirit of God, they are the sons of God. For ye have not received the spirit of bondage again to fear; but ye have received the Spirit of adoption, whereby we cry, Abba, Father. The Spirit itself beareth witness with our spirit, that we are the children of God: And if children, then heirs; heirs of God, and joint-heirs with Christ; if so be that we suffer with him, that we may be also glorified together.

ROMANS 8:14–17 KJV

DECLARATION FOR YOUR LIFE

By living under the guidance of the Holy Spirit, I demonstrate the fact that I am a son/daughter of God. The Holy Spirit is not in me to put me in bondage or make me afraid, but to bring me to the realization of my new relationship with my heavenly Father. The Holy Spirit bears witness with my own spirit that I am God's own son/daughter. It is through His revelation that I have realized that God is my Father. I am an actual heir in the royal family of God! I am God's own son/daughter and I share in the same inheritance that Jesus does! When I become one with Him in His suffering, I also become one with Him in His glory!

GOD CARES ABOUT DETAILS!

hortly after Mike and his wife became Christians, the IRS asked him to defend a tax return from years earlier. Unfortunately, he hadn't been honest, and so began months of painful meetings with the IRS.

The day of the last meeting, after parking, Mike discovered the meter wouldn't take his coins. He was already late, and he prayed, *Lord, I'm trusting You for a huge tax problem. It's dumb not to trust you with this little meter.*

When he came out later, he saw a piece of paper on his car. Stunned, he prayed, *Lord, I asked for Your help!* But when he came closer he saw a note from a friend: "Mike, your time was expired. I took care of it."

God cares about every detail of your life—from the big things to the smallest. Trust His loving-kindness to care for you throughout the day in every situation that you face.

What is man that you are mindful of him,
  the son of man that you care for him?
You made him a little lower than the
    heavenly beings
  and crowned him with glory and honor.
You made him ruler over the works of
    your hands;
  you put everything under his feet.

PSALM 8:4–6

DECLARATION FOR YOUR LIFE

*God is ever-mindful of me and cares for me with
unwavering diligence. He has created me to be just
short of divine (Elohim; God; heavenly beings) and
has crowned me with glory and honor.*

ne day a judge came into his doctor's office. The doctor asked what he was really there for because his leg cast didn't need to be checked.

He said, "I just thought that maybe you could give me a reason to live." He broke down and cried, and then the doctor led him to the Lord.

When the doctor asked what had prompted the man to come into his office and make such a cry for help, he said, "When you walked into the room, I saw something in your eyes that told me you had what I wanted. Something told me you knew the answer to life. I look into men's faces all day long, judging the truth. I could see that you believed with all your heart that what you were telling me was true. It was enough to convince me I needed it."

Just like this doctor, you can be a witness to others of the love of God. You have been chosen to be a witness in your sphere of influence. You are called to be a light in the world.

[Jesus said], "Let your light shine before
men in such a way that they may
see your good works, and glorify
your Father who is in heaven."

MATTHEW 5:16 NASB

DECLARATION FOR YOUR LIFE

*I am the light of the world. I will not hide my light,
but set it out where all can see it. I live my life in moral
excellence and with good, praiseworthy, and notable
deeds. I see to it that men recognize what God is doing
in my life so that they can give His name the honor
that it deserves.*

hen we are empowered by the Holy Spirit, we will be able to take the message of the Lord Jesus to the world. God is looking for imperfect men and women who have learned to walk in moment-by-moment dependence on the Holy Spirit—Christians who have learned to overcome their inadequacies, fears, and failures— believers who have become discontent with merely "surviving" and have taken the time to investigate everything God has to offer in this life.

God's method for reaching this generation and every generation is not preachers and sermons. It is Christians like you, who have been chosen to demonstrate His love to the world, whose lifestyles are empowered and directed by the Holy Spirit.

And Jesus came and spake unto them, saying, All power is given unto me in heaven and in earth. Go ye therefore, and teach all nations, baptizing them in the name of the Father, and of the Son, and of the Holy Ghost: Teaching them to observe all things whatsoever I have commanded you: and, lo, I am with you alway, even unto the end of the world. Amen.

MATTHEW 28:18–20 KJV

DECLARATION FOR YOUR LIFE

In Jesus—as His ambassador, brother/sister, and friend—I have been given the authority of heaven while on this earth. Jesus is always with me. He has given me His word that He will never leave me nor forsake me even to the end of the age.

he word *salvation* means "nothing missing, nothing broken; to be whole." Wholeness from God's perspective is to be complete; to know with deep assurance that we are beloved by God with an everlasting, infinite, and unconditional love; to be able to move forward with boldness and confidence in the knowledge that we are God's chosen children; to claim God's promises that we are victors through Christ Jesus over every negative situation and circumstance; and to be able to stand up to the enemy of our souls regardless of what the devil may throw at us.

Wholeness is the work that God does in you with a twofold purpose: that you might be sound in your spirit, mind, body, and emotions, and that you might influence others to accept God's love, forgiveness, and plan.

[Jesus said], "A thief is only there to steal and kill and destroy. I came so they can have real and eternal life, more and better life than they ever dreamed of."

JOHN 10:10 THE MESSAGE

DECLARATION FOR YOUR LIFE

I know that the thief comes only to steal, kill, and destroy. Jesus, on the other hand, came to give me the life of God with all of its abundance (provision overflowing and bursting through the seams).

For Such a Time as This

ed Engstrom once wrote of a Christian businessman from America who was traveling to various mission fields of the world. One day he found himself in India near a leprosarium. Outside of its walls he saw an unusual sight: a lovely young missionary attending the needs of a filthy leprous beggar. The man paused at the sight, then withdrew a few feet. Tears filled his eyes, and he said to the young nurse, "Young lady, I wouldn't do that for a million dollars." To which she replied, "Neither would I."

Oswald Chambers once said, "One man or woman called to God is worth a hundred who have elected to work for God."[2] God has called each of us to be His light in this world. Like the young missionary nurse, you, too, have a calling to fulfill. You have been chosen, and when you live out your purpose in life, the satisfaction you will feel will be worth more than all the money in the world.

"Who knows but that you have come to royal position for such a time as this?"

ESTHER 4:14

DECLARATION FOR YOUR LIFE

God chose me for a specific purpose. In His infinite wisdom, He has placed me in His kingdom for such a time as this. I am His ideal choice to carry out what He has called me to do. He has given me a mission to fulfill and I intend to fulfill it.

Walk in the Light

uring World War II, the island of Crete in the Mediterranean was invaded by the Nazis. As German paratroopers rained out of the sky onto the fields of Crete, they were gunned down.

The retribution was terrible. The Germans lined up whole villages of people and gunned them down. In the end, hatred was the only weapon the Cretan people had. They vowed to never give up their hatred. Never.

Yet now, on the site where the paratroopers landed, there is an institute where people come to learn about Greek culture and political harmony and peace. Why? Because of Dr. Alexander Papaderos, whose influence has changed his community.

During the War, he was only a boy. One day, on the road, he found the broken pieces of a mirror. A German motorbike had crashed there. He tried to find all the pieces and reassemble the mirror, but he couldn't. So he kept the largest piece, scratched it on a rock until it was round, and played with it as a toy. It became a game to reflect light into the most inaccessible places. Papaderos says: "I came to understand that this was not just a child's game, but what I might do with my life. I am a fragment of a mirror of God's love. I can reflect light into the dark places of this world."

Like Papaderos, you have been chosen to shine God's light in the world!

If we walk in the light, God himself being the light, we also experience a shared life with one another, as the sacrificed blood of Jesus, God's Son, purges all our sin.

1 John 1:7 The Message

DECLARATION FOR YOUR LIFE

I have been called into fellowship with God and with His Son, Jesus Christ. God is Light and in Him is no darkness at all. I am in Him. I walk in the Light, as He is in the Light. In doing so, I maintain fellowship with all of my brothers and sisters in Christ, and the blood of Jesus, the Son of God, cleanses me from all sin.

NOTES

1 Tony Evans, "Liberating Grace," *Decision*, July 2002, 25.

2 Oswald Chambers, *Disciples Indeed* (London: Morgan & Scott, 1955), 10.

PRAYER OF SALVATION

God loves you—no matter who you are, no matter what your past. God loves you so much that He gave His one and only begotten Son for you. The Bible tells us that "...whoever believes in him shall not perish but have eternal life" (John 3:16). Jesus laid down His life and rose again so that we could spend eternity with Him in heaven and experience His absolute best on earth. If you would like to receive Jesus into your life, say the following prayer out loud and mean it from your heart.

Heavenly Father, I come to You admitting that I am a sinner. Right now, I choose to turn away from sin, and I ask You to cleanse me of all unrighteousness. I believe that Your Son, Jesus, died on the cross to take away my sins. I also believe that He rose again from the dead so that I might be forgiven of my sins and made righteous through faith in Him. I call upon the name of the Lord Jesus Christ to be the Savior and Lord of my life. Jesus, I choose to follow You and ask that You fill me with the power of the Holy Spirit. I declare that right now I am a child of God. I am free from sin and full of the righteousness of God. I am saved in Jesus' name.

If you prayed this prayer to receive Jesus Christ as your Savior for the first time, please contact us on the Web at **www.harrisonhouse.com** to receive a free book.

Or you may write to us at

Harrison House
P.O. Box 35035
Tulsa, Oklahoma 74153

Discover the peace and power of knowing you are *Adored by God.*

There is a quiet confidence that comes when we know without a shadow of a doubt that we are loved by our gracious heavenly Father.

But too often, in the tumultuous experiences of life—strained relationships, too many responsibilities with not enough time, and any personal failings—we lose our sense of being cherished, of being unconditionally loved by God.

Adored by God is a simple yet poignant daily reminder that no matter what is happening in your world, the One who created you and who knows you best, is the One who loves you the very most!

Adored by God • 1-57794-802-5

Available at bookstores everywhere or visit **www.harrisonhouse.com**.